IT'S JUST A PHASE

TANISHA KITHANIYA

You know how it is. You pick up a book, flip to the dedication, and find that, once again, the author has dedicated a book to someone else and not to you.

Not this time.

Because we haven't yet met/have only a glancing acquaintance/are just crazy about each other/haven't seen each other in much too long/are in some way related/will never meet, but will, I trust, despite that, always think fondly of each other

This one's for you.

With you know what, and you probably know why.

Contents

The Introduction

My book is to inspire and motivate all readers that if they are going through a bad phase then don't loose your hopes because the best moments are yet to come! The things you are experiencing are just temporary as nothing is permanent in this entire world. This phrase "It's just a phase" is very close to my heart as I always feel that the bad time will get over at some point of time. There is a calming ring to the phrase "It's just a phase" because it implies a short-term obstacle/challenge/negative experience, which will actually come to an end very soon. Hope you like this book and get your hopes high!

1

A PIECE OF MOTIVATION

The biggest problem of this generation is that they think that "this is the end" but they are wrong.

It is truly said that "There is nothing permanent except change." You have to accept what is going on, face it, learn from it, get experience and MOVE ON!

Be it your work, career, circumstances or relationships, nothing is permanent, and everything keeps changing.

That particular emotion will not stay forever with you. Problems are like a test in front of you taken by God, if you succeed the god rewards you but if you don't then you learn and get experience, for the learning part and for your patience you still get rewarded.

You just have to keep your physical and mental health bold enough so that you can fight any problem or obstacles in this world.

Here, I love the example of the moon,

One day it's so happy and full of joy, shining bright in the sky

but the other day it disappears and is very sad and dull.

That doesn't mean it will stop shining and lose hopes,

it comes, shrinks,disappears, increases and then is full!

It means that the moon's phases aren't fixed, here positions mean emotions. It changes! Even the moon itself says "It's just a phase, it will pass."

It's easy to say that "chill, move on!" but the one who implies it and moves on, is the true champion!

Now about the change, Change is hard to be made but very beautiful when made!

See the butterflies, they come out from a cocoon.

They have to make a change but when the change is made, it is exquisite!

Just go on with the life process and trust it.

Peace should be your priority. Make deliberate life choices to protect your mental, emotional and spiritual

state.

By becoming better prove yourself to yourself,not to others!

Be proud of yourself!

Always remember "Self-love is not selfish yet it is very important"

As long as you are self-confident, nothing in the entire world can stop you.

The biggest enemy of self-confidence is self-doubt.

Having self-doubts and insecurities let you down. So just be chill and let the world say whatever it wants to!

It's true that taking suggestions is indeed, but at last, do what your heart wants!

Never be afraid to take a different path from others. Who knows, maybe that different path you chose will be an inspiration to others one day!

Don't compare yourselves from others, each one of you is different and is idiosyncratic in their own way!

We all know that diverse kinds of flowers make a gorgeous and colourful garden! Just like that individuals with different talents and skills make a glamorous world all together.

One more problem is that we all tend to brag about our future goals, start telling to everyone.

According to me, one should not tell their plans to everyone, instead show them your results and leave them flabbergast.

2

Uff...the negative thoughts!

The negative thoughts we have in our minds while going through a rough phase are not in our control.

The thoughts just come and bother us. Those negative thoughts force us to do something unwilling.

We have to fight with those thoughts and win over them, these negative thoughts are just like storms that blow in our minds.

If one is fragile in body and even in mind, one can be destroyed and broken down easily.

On the other hand, if one is strong and bold enough to handle the situations can fight the hardships and the storms of life.

The negative thoughts of hurting yourself and suiciding are just not worth it!

Just remember if you are still alive then you are alive for a reason. So, find out that reason and make yourself better each day!

I don't like to be the best every day, I like to make myself better with every coming day so that one day I can call myself the best!

That's what even you should believe in!

We can also compare negative thoughts to a flowing river, the flowing rivers are our negative thoughts and we are in the boat. If we are prepared and we know how to escape and not just be restless, we win.

But if we are just scared of the fact that we will die and can do nothing, we will fall and face failure.

It's still fine to fail because we learn from our mistakes and get experience, but doing that same mistake every time and not even trying is not good.

Learn to be satisfied with whatever you have because the life you are living now, is also a dream of millions. So always be satisfied with your life. Be happy in every moment of life!

Believe in sudden positive shifts. Things can change for you at any time. Trust that.

There are two ways to be happy: Change the situation or change your mindset towards it.

Life can be simple but we make it more complicated by overthinking and over analyzing.

The answers we seek, never come when the mind is busy, they come when the mind is still.

Mindset is everything, Mindset is a superpower given to each one of us. Power can either be destructing or peaceful, and should know how to use it wisely.

Stop worrying about people who are not worried about you.

Just remember "it's a phase" and it will pass. Just don't give a damn about it!

3

Do whatever you admire!

Now to distract yourself from the troubling thoughts, do something don't be idle because when you are doing nothing, you tend to overthink everything!

Just do whatever you like, I know it will be hard to get out of your comfort zone but trust me, you will feel better than before.

First thing, be happy and then start! Keep all of your thoughts aside for a moment and start doing that particular activity you have selected.

When I feel anxious or maybe I having a rough day, then I write. I feel so much better when I write down my thoughts and then convert them into stories. I just love it! And most importantly I feel myself! I try to move on from that phase.

One can do meditation when not in the mood to do anything else. Play soft music, sit in an open place and just close your eyes and meditate!

If you are sad or depressed, don't let that show on your face. People who judge you and hate you, will be happy to see you in that state but your enemies should be in trouble when they see a huge smile on your face, they will be jealous of you and your life.

They would think that your life is perfect but deep inside you are fighting and not showing that outside. That is when you get mature.

Now jealousy, people often get jealous seeing others happy and start thinking that their life is perfect. But remember nobody's life is smooth like butter it's just that some people don't show it outside.

Happiness is a state of mind, it cannot be achieved. It can only be experienced. Happiness is already within you, you just have to find out that happiness inside you.

Again I would like to say that think about what you like to do and don't talk yourself into something for fear of being left out. That being said, it's important to try different things. Push yourself out of your comfort zone and you may surprise yourself in the end.

What others think is their business. It's your birthright to do things you love.

Choose a particular thing to do every day, like reading.

Then make it a habit then your lifestyle. It takes 21 days to make it a habit and 90 days to turn it into a lifestyle.

Discipline and being consistent is very important to reach success and your goals.

And finally, laugh a lot, laugh till your tummy hurts and water starts coming out of your eyes!

4

We are fighters! We can fight this!

Life is a fight, we all are fighters,and we all have it inside. We are fighting every second of our lives, but most of the time we do not notice it.

Tough times don't last. Tough people do. We are fighters, when we get down, we will get back up.

Say this to yourself every day:

I am a fighter, I will not give up, I will stumble and I will fall but I will stand back up. It might take longer at times but I WILL stand up and keep fighting.

Everyone should be a fighter, not a quitter.

A true warrior accepts the challenges of life in true humility. No matter what his destiny may be, it can never be a cause for discontent, but a living challenge which it is his privilege to surmount.

You have to fight through some bad days to earn the best days of your life.

Out of every one hundred people, ten should not even be there, eighty are just targets, nine are the real fighters and we are lucky to have them, for they make the battle. Ah, but the one, one is a warrior, and that one will bring the others back.

We can do anything we want to as long as we give it everything we have got.

Each new day is a blessing. Let go of worries and be grateful for all the positives in your life.

And listen, yes you, the one reading this book, soon things will be brighter!

Remember IT'S JUST A PHASE!

Thank You For Reading My Book!

Thank you for reading my book. I hope you liked it and will prefer this to others.

"We all have phases we go through in life. It is not always possible to be emotionally, physically, mentally and spiritually balanced and primed all the time...and it's okay to not be okay. You will find your way"

www.ingramcontent.com/pod-product-compliance
Lightning Source LLC
Chambersburg PA
CBHW022048150726
47990CB00004B/1648

FOREWORD BY PROPHET ISAAC ANTO

PROPHETIC PRAYER GUIDE

Strategic Prayer Topics To Transform
Your Prayer Life...

JAMES OWUSU

III

DEDICATION

To my lovely wife Mrs Deborah Owusu and my children, Richardson, Juanita, James, and Melchizedek.

Now to you the reader, without you this has no meaning and impact.

ACKNOWLEDGEMENT

I am grateful to the Almighty God for He has been faithful to me and His promises come to pass when we believe them.

My special thanks to my biological parents Rev. James Afram Owusu Snr. and Late Prophetess Alice Owusu and to my siblings.

Also to everyone who made this possible.

CONTENTS

FOREWORD

Prayer is a communication between man and God. For one to pray prophetically to receive answers you will definitely need a guide.

This book has been written to guide us pray effectively and transform our prayer life. It touches on deep prophetic topics and directions that will help us receive rapid answers for our prayers.

May God answer you speedily as you use this guide. Amen!

Prophet Isaac Anto
[General Overseer, Conqueros Chapel International]

INTRODUCTION

When prayers are effective heaven accepts and answers. A Christian who want to fulfill his/her God-given purpose on earth can't do without prayer, as the Bible say; ***"Men ought to pray"*** (Luke 18:1).

Prayer is a force of power and when held on to, our lives becomes untouchable to the enemy and immune to the norms of the world. As it was in the times of old, prayer itself has not changed, it does not change but has been a divinely force that causes bad situations to change.

As taught to the disciples by Jesus in Luke

14:2-4; it is important for every Christian to pray, and also how to prayer whether a beginner or a matured one. For prayer to be effective it must be said in the right way. You need to know the Word of God; it takes only the Word to empower your prayer life.

There is a word which has been prophesied into your life waiting to be manifested in time but for lack of prayer the devil has taken an advantage of your laziness to frustrate and hinder that blessing. Remember when you don't pray enough you become a play tool for the devil.

There are some situations you might not know how to pray or which direction to go but this book is meant to help you grow both spiritually and naturally in order to overcome the traps of the enemy at any time.

Until prayers are made, blessings are hindered and the answers we seek to find are not delivered. Prayers can also empower our angels to work for us.

Prayer sometimes comes in the form of a command, request, petition or a decree. To every situation there is a particular time and weapons to use. This master piece will make you a winner and guide you to transform your unwanted situations.

"When your prayer is effective, heaven accepts your them."

"Until prayers are made, blessings are hindered."

PRAYER POINTS

THE GRACE OF GOD

Grace is incomparable, there is nothing beyond it and you can't change grace. (See 1 Cor. 15:9-10)

- Holy Ghost as I pray and declare let your grace qualify me, to where I've been disqualified and to do what I can't do.

For everything good there is an evil will to destroy it. When you don't have the power of God in you; you give the devil an advantage over yourself. (See Luke 10:19)

- Lord as I pray, take me to a level of power that I can thread upon the serpents and scorpions (devil) working tirelessly to destroy every good thing in my life.

- Lord by prayer, empower me to overcome every obstacle of the devil; and to change to my life's position.
- Lord empower me to mount up wings like eagle to penetrate through every problem I'm been faced with.
- Anyone with the tongue of a scorpion who is poisoning my destiny by the power of God, I thread upon them and take over.

God respects and values blood so as the devil. Behind every blood there is a spirit, and blood draws attention. (See Gen. 4:1-10)

- *(Pour the blood, Communion wine)* Lord consecrate this communion and as I take it consecrate my blood and let your spirit be with me.

- Lord consecrate my life and my blood through the blood of Jesus.
- Lord as I have taken the blood let your spirit back me in everything I do from now onwards.
- Lord as I open my mouth in prayer by the release of your blood question my enemies.
- Lord by your blood restore unto me anything good that has come out of my life.

Using the blood of Jesus as a weapon (See 2 Cor 10:3-5, Rev. 4:11)

- Lord as I pray and clap my hands whoever or any demon living in my life as a Goliath by the power of the blood I cut off his head.

- As I pray Lord, I battle every witchcraft in my family by the blood of Jesus; as I clap my hands in prayer, I destroy them.
- In the name of Jesus, I kill every evil person or witch against my job, marriage, finances, happiness and family; with the blood, I poison every witchcraft meeting against me and my household.

The blood changes sweat to sweet and resurrect any dead thing *(Sprinkle the blood (communion wine) in your house)*
- As I clap my hands in prayer who ever has taken me to a spiritualist to destroy me by the blood of Jesus I bury you.
- Every door the devil uses as a passage way into my life, by prayer I shut it with the blood of Jesus.

- As I sprinkle the blood of Jesus in my house and the area I live, whoever is destroying any good thing coming into my life be destroyed by the blood.

Pick 3 Stones; (See Ephesians 6:12, 1 John 5:4)
- Lord I consecrate these stones with the blood of Jesus as I lift up my voice in prayer.
- Any strong man in my life be it my mother, father or friend, Lord as I open my mouth to pray let them be hit by the stone as I throw it; by the blood fall and die.
- Lord as I lift up my voice in prayer any strong man who has turned him/herself into an animal let him/her be hit by the stone when I throw it and kill them by the power of the Blood.

- Anyone working to spoil my identity to turn my helpers away as I throw the stone hit them and make them fall sick to the point of death by the Blood.
- Good accept my prayer and assign angles for my prayers to bring it to pass in Jesus name.

NB: After prayers throw the stone away between 12am and 2am.

Pour the blood on sand and put your right foot on it, mark your fore head with the blood and drink a little of it.

- Lord as I pray and stand on this sand I break every evil foundation in my family working against my destiny by the power of the Blood. Jesus as I stand on this land I go into my family, by this direction. However, those foundations were built by the power of a blood, I break down the evil foundations.

- Any foundation of the place I stay working against my wealth, job, children, health, education, marriage as a clap my hands and pray standing on the sand, I destroy it in the name of Jesus.

- Lord as I clap my hands and pray anyone who has cursed me by pouring oil, water, egg or any substance on the ground, whatever he or she said and did on the earth as I stand on this sand with prayer I reverse it in Jesus name.

NB: Pour the sand on 3 different places and live a little for keep and every once in a month pray with it.

When God is coming down with a blessing He will not give you beyond

*your expectations. **When you are rejected pursue God**.* (See 1 Sam. 1:5-19)

- Oh Lord, any right person I need to be connected to, direct me to meet them. Whether they are in my life or not cause us to meet by your grace and power.

EXERCISING HEAVENLY COMMAND

The language of heaven is prayer. When you don't have the word of God your prayer becomes weak. Prayer is the only thing that can cause a situation to change. (See 2 Kings 20:1-6, 1 Kings 8:1, John 1:12)

- Lord give me the spirit of prayer.
- Lord as I open my mouth in prayer disgrace any witchcraft that is fighting against me publicly .
- Anyone who has planted evil charm to destroy me, Lord by your power as I

pray take it out.

- Any evil plot of the evil one against me to waste my resources through sickness or any problem Lord, as I pray by your power let the earth swallow him or her up.
- Lord as I clap my hands and pray, I burn any written book of poverty concerning my family against my prosperity; BURN BY FIRE!
- Lord as I pray any goodness my family and friends didn't do for me let strangers do it for me in Jesus name.
- Lord as I clap my hands and pray by your power give me a 360° turning point of miracle in my life.

If you know how to pray God will answer you. God provides according to your prayers. Man's will cannot bring a change

to God's will. (See Matt. 6:9)

- Spirit of the living God arise and take me to my place of blessing.
- Lord through my prayer connect, correct and direct my helpers to me in Jesus name.

Faith is the evidence of what God will do to the current situation. People of faith talk less and pray more. (Zech 9:11, Lev. 17:11, Heb 11:1)

- Jesus as I clap my hands and pray and drink the blood may your covenant in the Blood speak for me.
- Jesus by the covenant of the Blood I set my life free from any evil covenant.
- Lord any witch or person who is holding my blessing and preventing my happiness, Lord I stand by your blood let that person be destroyed and

I possess my possessions.

NB: Pour the blood on the ground

- (Read Ps. 56:6) Oh Lord in this month, previous and ahead, anywhere I have been to and I will go to, that there will be a bad report, Lord by fire speak for me.

- Oh Lord, I go for any backdated prophecy and blessing by faith I manifest them.

- I declare, I refuse poverty, divorce, sickness. I will build my future with my own words as I pray by fire.

- Any spirit assigned to destroy me concerning my future as I clap my hands and pray I release the fire of God upon you.

- Any spirit of fear planted in my body and soul as I clap my hands and pray I declare any fear to come out by fire.

- Oh Lord! As I clap my hands and pray release angelic assistance as I journey into my future.
- Oh Lord! Give me the mantle of prayer that fell on Elijah, give me fire to pray.

MINISTRATION OF THE ANGELS

Every one needs an angel and everyone has an angel. Angels don't work for the one who does not know the word of God. They work in the spiritual and it takes place in the natural. (See Ps. 8:5, Heb 1:4)

- Jesus as I pray release my angel.
- Lord give me an angel as you have purposed for my destiny that the plans of the enemy will be revealed to me.
- Lord let my angel to go to my destiny helpers and to remind them of me in the name of Jesus.

HOW TO PUT YOUR ANGELS TO WORK

Angels move according to the word of God. You put them to work through the knowledge of God, confidence by conviction and through prayer you command them. (See Dan 3:16-18)

- Lord through prayer release the angels that you have assigned for my life.

- Lord as I open my mouth in prayer I send angels to everywhere my enemies have gathered concerning my joy, health, job, finance, marriage, family; let your angels destroy them.

- Lord as I clap and pray, angels of my life I command you to take out any bad thing the enemy have deposited into my life; angels by my prayer take it out of my life.

- Angels take me to my place of

elevation, prosperity, breakthrough as I clap my hands and pray.

- Angels go to my helpers and give them sleepless nights until they have helped me as I open my mouth to pray.

VICTORY OVER FINANCIAL HANDICAP

It is never the will of God for you to be poor. The poor hasn't got a voice not even a choice. If you are poor you can never expose the wisdom of God. (Mal 3:8-9, Luke 6:38, Gen. 8:22)

- Lord quicken my spirit to be yielded with ideas to create wealth in Jesus name.
- Lord as I pray cause my finances to be too hot for my enemy to touch it.
- Lord impact unto me the grace of giving.

Giving + Working = God's prosperity. Money has a voice, it makes people powerful and influential. (See Ecc 9:14, 4:12)

- Lord give me wisdom and ideas to locate where you have positioned my wealth, as I open my mouth and pray show me what to do.
- Lord wherever I am standing and people are laughing, saying evil things as a clap my hands and pray change my position according to their mockery.
- Lord as I clap and pray change my position for people to respect and serve you.

TIME AND DESTINY

If you know how to manage a situation in a period of time you receive a promotion anytime you force into a place where

you are not supposed to, you give the devil advantage over yourself. When you discover who you are, then you will know what you want.

- Oh Lord, as I pray by your spirit reveal to me who I am and what you have destined for me.

- Oh Lord strengthen me for every period I am in now and those who are ahead of me for the sake of my destiny, Lord impact unto me wisdom to manage my period so that I can take care of my period.

- Lord as I clap and pray empower me to walk according to the timing of my destiny and whatever will be a stumbling block by your power I take it out.

- Lord take me out from human timing, any managing life which is human timing, Lord Jesus as I lift up my voice in prayer in prayer take me out.

- Oh Lord as I pray, into my future whatever the devil has planned against me; when I am getting closer Lord direct my path, that I will not fall prey to it.
- Oh Lord as I pray break every ignorance of my age against your timing in Jesus name.
- Lord as I pray help me to walk in your timing, reveal yourself unto me so that I can be able to do what's needed to get closer to you.

Every name has got its assignment and problems to solve. Your name has a connection to you destiny. (See Luke 1:15-16)

- Any negative result attached to my

name, Lord by your blood I disconnect my name and life from that negativity in Jesus name.

- Oh Lord as I lift my voice up in prayer under any demonic meeting they mention my name by your power let fire appear.

- Lord as I pray I need your love to connect my name anywhere I go, where by whoever hears my name or sees it will be of help to me.

- Oh Lord as I pray, usher my name into my destiny that on this earth I can be able to walk into my place of purpose, where I belong. Any demonic hindrance preventing me from entering into my destiny Lord as I pray usher me in; in Jesus' name.

The power of God has a potential to

transform. What makes the Holy Spirit to be what He is; is the availability of Power and you receive a miracle based on the level of power you operate in God. (See Acts 1:8)

- Holy Ghost as I clap my hands and pray I ask for power to succeed, to attract wealth and to move forward in everything I do in my life.

- Lord by your power I disconnect myself from any negative person in my life and bring good people my way.

- Lord I stand by the power and grace upon your servant the Prophet that whoever has poured any substance or buried anything in the ground against me to bring my downfall, Lord as I clap my hands and pray let the power over his life connect with that evil cause and destroy them completely.

- Holy Spirit manifest your power in my family, life concerning my marriage, children, health, finance, business and every area of my life.

(Write your name and that of your children, siblings on a paper and pour the blood (communion wine) on it. Pray and bath with the blood for three (3) days and after burn the paper.) Names are revealing and agenda fulfilling.

- Lord connect my name into your purpose and reveal unto me the revelation behind my name.
- Any name given to me that has taken effect negatively on my life Lord as I have taken in your blood let your blood deliver me.
- Lord I connect my name to the Spirit of God and let your spirit connect my

name to the revelation behind my name as I pray may you reveal why I was given this name.

- Lord anytime my name is been mentioned let the blessing in my name appear both in the kingdom of light and darkness, spiritual and physical where and whenever it is mentioned let success appear.

Prayer makes one great and brings you closer unto God. God don't hide His revelation unto the prayerful. Prayer brings down the Kingdom of God. (See Jer. 33:3) *(Use a towel [white], anoint it with oil and perfume and make it a prayer mantle with faith.)*

- Lord as the prayer mantle is upon me impact unto me the spirit of prayer
- Lord let the counsel of the devil

against my future, marriage, home, travelling, education be frustrated as I lift up prayer.

- Lord as I clap my hands and pray any evil door opened by any member of my family before me Holy Ghost by your power I shut that door
- Lord as I open my mouth in prayer, I break and loose myself from any satanic bondage.
- All evil broadcast to destroy me Lord as I pray and clap my hands let it turn for my testimony.
- Oh Lord as I open my mouth to pray; Lord provide for my helpers to help me.
- Lord by prayer turn my sweat and pain into blessings and joy.
- Lord make me a giver who has no pity for money as I pray.

- Lord by prayer I want to hear your voice concerning my life

Every enemy has a wicked thought and will not be happy or comfortable to see you move ahead in life. When you are not in the spirit you give the devil and your enemy advantage over you life. If you are not prayerful to fight with the enemy, he will always destroy your life. (See Psalm 3:7) [use the prayer mantle]

- Lord as I clap and pray any evil seed planted in my life I uproot it the same way it was planted in Jesus name.
- Any covenant someone has entered into which is evil that as long as they live I won't progress, as the prayer mantle is on me with prayer Lord I break that covenant.
- Lord as I lift up my voice in prayer

disgrace anyone who has accepted to be a witch because of me.

- Lord as I pray by your power I command my glory to come out from any evil cage.
- Lord mark my life with success, blessings, promotion, progress, joy, peace, good health, as I lift up my hands and pray mark me Lord.

BREAKING LIMITATIONS;

When you are limited you are not respected, you don't be in charge, you don't have a voice; that makes you controlled. You remain stagnant in a particular place for long. Problems are ladder for limitation to rule your life.

- Jesus as I lift up my voice in prayer any limitation in my family against my finances as I pray I break that limitation in Jesus name.

- Any problem that the witches in my family are using to limit me in life Holy Spirit as I lift up my voice in prayer I destroy that problem by the power of the blood of Jesus.

- Any witchcraft, fetish priest manipulation behind my limitation be it family curse, evil covenant as I pray, Holy Spirit I break those limitations in Jesus name.

- Lord connect me to my Peter to lift me out of my limitation concerning my travelling, finance, marriage, job, health and every area of my life.

ARRESTING SATANIC WICKEDNESS;
The devil or enemy is not friendly. (See John 10:10, Job 1:13-22)

- Jesus any spirit who has taken a

contract against me, as I pray Lord, I destroy that contract by fire.

- Any secret meeting going on against me to collapse every good thing in the camp of the enemy, as I pray I destroy that meeting and release fire of the Holy Ghost, I destroy their agenda in Jesus name.
- Oh Lord! Let every move of the enemy be put to stop by your power and grace now and today as I pray.
- As I lift up my voice to pray Lord make my life and every good thing of mine untouchable that nobody can stop me
- Lord ordain my life to attract goodness and make me attractive in the sight of helpers, husband/wife, to financial breakthrough as I lift up my voice in prayer in the name of Jesus.

THE COUNSEL OF THE LORD

It is not what you know or think that will decide your destiny. You are a vessel and when you are able to walk in the right path the Lord delivers you and your generation. When you walk with God and submit to Him you enjoy his provision (See Prov. 19:21, Kings 7:18)

- Holy Spirit as I lift my hands and pray I need your divine direction to establish my life.

Fruitfulness brings attention and direct people out of barrenness. Fruitfulness has it root in the word of God. Barrenness is satanic and it difficult for people to trust you with success and get connected to you. (See Gen 1:22 – 28) *[Take an apple and consecrate it with the blood of Jesus]*

- Oh Lord! By this prophetic direction

as I pray and eat this fruit I uproot any spirit of barrenness out of my life.

- Lord any satanic activity that is causing barrenness in my life, be it in my marriage, job, finances, family, education, health by this prophetic direction Lord I uproot it.

- Any curse operation in my family that is programming barrenness in my life by this prophetic direction I rebuke and uproot that curse.

- Oh Lord! Open my new chapter of fruitfulness as I do this prophetic direction *(new chapter brings new ideas, relationship, business opportunities).*

The blood never fails in any situation. [Drink communion wine and anoint yourself].

- Lord as I have taken in the blood, let your life in the blood, enter into me to take away sickness, poverty and shame in Jesus name.
- Lord as I have taken in the blood come down from your throne and enter into the camp of my enemy and destroy them as I lift my voice in prayer.
- I disconnect my blood from any bloodline of my family (mother and father) Lord as I have taken in your blood.
- I mark myself with the blood for my life to be untouchable, Holy Ghost as I pray and declare by the release of the blood, witches in my family you can't pursue me, I have marked myself with the blood and I am untouchable, my business, health, travelling and every aspect of my life.

THE BLOOD

Divine provision for mans' freedom. (See Exodus 12:21-28) ***The blood was released for the freedom of God's children but for the destruction and punishment of the enemy. The Blood of Jesus is a weapon.***
[Take your communion wine]

- Lord by faith, I turn this wine into the blood of Jesus, as I use it let there be a manifestation of miracle in my life. *[After; drink and anoint yourself with the blood]*

- Lord as I have taken and applied the blood, I need freedom in my life, marriage, job, family, health as I pray in the name of Jesus.

- Lord as I have applied the blood send forth your angel of death into the camp of my enemy to attack them. Any witch or any person who has sent me to a place for my life to be destroyed Jesus as I open my mouth to pray send your angel as you did to the Egyptians.

- Oh Lord by your blood release unto me my miracles and anybody or spirit, witch holding my miracle by the power of the Blood release it. I declare unto you release my success, promotion, money as I pray in the name of Jesus.

OH LORD LET MY BLESSINGS FLOW!

If you want to walk in the blessings of God focus on God only and put man aside for man is used by God. The blessings of God are reflective and advertise you in the sight of greatness. People are custodians to the manifestation of God's blessings for your life. (See Eph. 1:3, Prov. 10:22, Ps. 68:9)

- Oh Lord! Connect me to the right person who has my blessings as I open my mouth to pray in Jesus name.

- Oh Lord! In the name of Jesus, as I open my mouth in prayer let my blessings in the hands of people be released into my life.

- Holy Ghost as I pray, all my blessings which has been scattered, locate me, blessing of my marriage, business, by prayer let it locate me now in Jesus name.

- My father, my father, as I pray connect me to the people who will bless me, financially, business wise and every area of my destiny.

- My father my father, any enemy of my blessings in my family, community, work, village as I lift my voice in prayer, die in the name of Jesus.

ABOUT THE AUTHOR

Prophet James Owusu is a Christian statesman, advisor to leaders, father to many, and a mentor to a number of Christian leaders who has submitted to his prophetic grace.

He is the President of James Owusu Ministries; a ministry which seeks to cause liberation to people from all walks of life, discover and direct destinies through the prophetic ministry.

He is happily married to the Mrs. Deborah Owusu and they are blessed with four wonderful children.

Get Connected

- James Owusu
- Prophet James Owusu
- Prophet James Owusu
- +233 244087189
- jamesowusuministries@gmail.com